To Donald

Yes God Can!

K

Yes, I Can

Set My House In Order! ™

Your Guide To Building A Financially Successful Life

written by

Keith Carter, RFC, MBA

To learn more about "Yes, I Can Set My House in Order," order more copies of this book or schedule Keith for workshops or speaking events, contact Keith Carter at:
6440 Avondale Drive, Suite 200, Oklahoma City, OK 73116
1-888-580-0937 or 405-330-6431

Book designed by Sean Love :: www.The-LoveGroup.com

ISBN - 10: 0615270883
ISBN - 13: 9780615270883

Table of Contents

Introduction

"Therefore whoever hears these sayings of Mine, and does them, I will liken him to a wise man who built his house on the rock: and the rain descended, the floods came, and the winds blew and beat on that house; and it did not fall, for it was founded on the rock.
"But everyone who hears these sayings of Mine, and does not do them, will be like a foolish man who built his house on the sand: and the rain descended, the floods came, and the winds blew and beat on that house; and it fell. And great was its fall" (Matthew 7:24-27).

God's words are clear about how He wants your house. He wants a house that will stand the test of time by having a good foundation and an aligned cornerstone. He doesn't want a house built on sand; He wants a house built on the rock.

He doesn't want your house shaking or cracked by poor finances. If you have your finances in order, your house can truly be a home.

But it's not easy to keep your finances in order. You must choose how you want to deal with finances in your home. You can choose stress or success. You can choose peace or chaos. You can work your entire life for nothing or for something.

You can say, "Yes, I Can Set My House in Order!"

Let's break down our title.

YES in this sense introduces a more emphatic or explicit phrase.

I means you can do it; your goals can be accomplished.

CAN means you *will* do it, not you *may* do it. You aren't asking permission. Instead, you have the ability to accomplish goals that are possible and probable.

In the book of Isaiah, the 38th chapter and the first verse, the Word says, *"In those days Hezekiah was sick and near death. And Isaiah the prophet, the son of Amoz, went to him and said to him, "Thus says the LORD: 'Set your house in order, for you shall die and not live.'"* Hezekiah was sick, and God instructed the prophet to tell him that he was going to die. Death is a reality in all our lives. But must we die while we are still living? When your house is stressed, you feel like death has come and taken your soul while your body is still living. Stress can literally suck the life from you.

God wants us to set our houses in order: make our houses strong; build our houses on Him, the solid rock; and start building brick by brick.

He wants us to start getting knowledge about how the financial world works; to have a place to store our income and dispense money to pay our bills; to make sure we protect our family, our property, and our lives; and to take advantage of any benefits offered by our employers.

He wants us to establish short- and long-term goals; to have a plan for death with estate planning; to organize our financial records; and to make budgeting a family event so that we can save for emergencies.

Next, we should manage our housing purchase by not buying too much house for our money, by minimizing the amount of money we pay for our transportation, and by living *within* our means – not beyond our means. Then, we should minimize taxes and manage emergencies as they come based on the fact that we have expected them and have not been surprised by them.

Next, we should eliminate our credit card debt card-by-card and get rid of all the installment loans that we have. As we build our financial house we should learn that saving and then buying is the best option rather than buying and then paying the creditor. We should also start investing in ourselves through education.

Lastly, we should start making money, not just from our paycheck but also from the money that we save from eliminating debt, making smarter purchases, mainly having a vision, all of which will allow us to invest. We should invest in mutual funds, stocks, bonds, and real estate and consider all investment options based on our vision and goals.

We are on a journey to build the house that God desires for us – a house that is set in order. Do you see the words *set in order*? That is what God wants in your life and what I want to give you with this book. I want to hear you shout with victory **"Yes, I Can Set My House in Order!"** It is a positive approach. You can make your goals and vision a reality!

But first, you need to get rid of the stress that most people are facing. Most people are just surviving and not thriving. They are late with payments. They avoid their mailbox because they know it will be stuffed with bills. Under the roof of their home is nothing but stress. Seven out of ten working families live paycheck to paycheck.

Their houses are out of order because their bricks and foundation are in the wrong place. Everything is off-center. The bills weigh more than the income. "Desire and Will to Succeed" are the cornerstone, but there is no action or knowledge to accompany it.

There is a better way. With this book, you can find your vision, action, and knowledge and make your topsy-turvy home level.

I will show you a life with more success and less stress – a way to stop living paycheck-to-paycheck and to plan for emergencies.

I will show you how to make your money work for you and how to leave behind the nightmare you're living and realize your dreams.

Read this book, and learn how to say with confidence, "Yes, I Can Set My House in Order!"

Chapter 1
It Begins With a Vision

Scripture teaches us that without vision, the people perish. Think about your vision right now. What kind of future do you want? What do you want to contribute to the world? What do you want your family and spiritual relationships to be like?

All of these areas are touched by the vision you have for yourself.

They are also touched by your finances. In fact, almost everything you choose to do requires money.

You need to create a vision for your life and for your money. It is not an easy task, but it can be a powerful tool in directing your life from one stage to another.

Your vision should touch every step you will read about in this book, starting with how you handle your finances. Do you use cash, or do you use credit cards? Are you diligent with your budget? All these actions come from your vision.

Most importantly, your financial vision should come from God.

God will give you a clear vision that allows you to make sense of your life. A vision can occur through a dream, a trance, or in the imagination. While a vision for your life may sound like a complicated concept, it can be easily broken down into three basic parts.

A Vision Comes *Before* Action

A vision will grow out of an idea, so you will need to understand your vision before you take any action. For example, imagine that you are getting ready to run a race: before you take your first step, you should envision yourself on the course, running and crossing the finish line. Then, you can run the race successfully because you have a vision. Having a vision *after* you've already run the race just doesn't make sense. That's why vision works with goals. As you envision your actions, you are able to set goals as well as the strategies to achieve them. Once you have envisioned your hopes, the actions required to turn those hopes into reality become clearer.

God Creates Your Vision

Don't worry that you may not have a vision for your life.

God has one for you already.

As you grow closer to Him, God will share that vision. That is God's nature. With your vision in your mind and your heart, you will move on with confidence. Remember all the attributes of God as you seek your vision.

God is eternal (Psalm 102:12). God knows all (1 Chronicles 28:9). God is unchanging (Malachi 3:6). God is holy (Psalm 99:9). God is just (Psalm 89:14). God is everywhere (Jeremiah 23:23-24). God is powerful (Isaiah 42:5). God is love (1 John 4:7).

God is all of these things, and He has a plan and a vision for you. Look for it. God can do so much for the world and so much for you.

A Vision Conveys a Revelation

A vision involves a truth being revealed. The Bible contains many instances of God revealing a vision. For instance, in Luke 1:27-38, an angel appears to Mary and reveals God's vision for her life: to bear the Son of God. At first Mary was unsure and asked the angel, "How shall this be?" The angel replied, "For with God nothing shall be impossible."

How will your vision be revealed? Mark 9:23 says, *"Jesus said to him, If you can believe, all things are possible to him who believes."*

All things are possible through God, and your belief in God's ability allows all things to be possible for you, including knowing and carrying out the vision He has for your life.

Shaping Your Vision

Where do you begin with your vision? First, you need to ask God that His will for your life be done and that you have the wisdom to accomplish it. Do you remember what James said in James 1:5? *"If any of you lacks wisdom, let him ask of God, who gives to all liberally and without reproach, and it will be given to him."*

Make sure that asking God is your first step and not your last resort.

God wants you to ask Him everything. Don't just ask Him about your vision but about all aspects of your life. Ask God to give you prudence to follow a worthwhile life vision.

Just like anything else, following a life vision comes from trial and error. YOU WILL MAKE MISTAKES ALONG THE WAY! But that's OK; don't become overwhelmed. God will be with you throughout this journey. If you get stuck, talk to God. If you have success, talk to God. Involve God in every step along the way.

A Vision That Works for Your Life

A vision for your life and your finances is personal and unique to you. God knows that, and you should know it, too.

How do you want to use your special talents and gifts for a life path that only you can fulfill?

A vision will give you the blueprint for carrying out your answers to that question – a blueprint that God has written just for you!

Working Toward Your Vision

Don't think that because your vision has been created by God, it's going to be easy. **It's not**. Your vision will require work. Action is required to achieve your life vision, and two specific types of action should be taken in order to develop your vision. First, you must incorporate your vision into your present life. You need to think about your vision throughout the day, running the important decisions that you make through your vision. Start comparing the tasks and activities of your everyday life with your life vision. For each of your activities, ask yourself, "Does this further my vision?" While many of your activities won't change, some of them will, and those changes will move you from the life you are living now (with debt and without a budget) to the life you want to lead (with more money, a better plan, and a brighter future).

The second action you must take is to bring your vision into your future.

The best way to take that action is to set goals. Setting goals is a very productive way to reinforce the positive changes in your life, as you will see in the course of this book.

In Acts 10, Peter's vision was revealed to him by God: to extend the fellowship of God's grace to non-Jews. Peter went to the rooftop to pray, and while he was praying he became very hungry. As he waited for the servants to prepare his meal, he fell into a trance. During this trance, Peter saw heaven open, and an object appeared in the distance. As it came closer, he noticed that the object looked like a sheet. The sheet opened to him, and out came many different types of animals. God told Peter, "Rise Peter, slay and eat," but Peter refused because the animals were common and unclean. This happened three times. God would say, "Rise, Peter, slay and eat," and Peter would say, "I refuse because the animals are unclean." Every time, God would say in response, "What I have cleansed, thou shall not call common."

After this vision, Peter realized that God's message for him was to spread the Word of God to non-Jews (Gentiles). Then Peter extended the Word of God to Cornelius, a Gentile. Peter's action lead to the extension of God's Word to all people, and it was only possible through Peter's obedience to his vision.

You may not understand God's vision at first. You may not even obey Him at first. But if you follow His vision for you and take action, you, your family, and your finances will never be the same again.

VISION EXERCISES

You are statistically more likely to achieve those things which you take the time to write down. Writing down answers to the following questions will help you to develop your life vision and goals.

What is my life vision?

____

____

____

What is my life vision for my family?

____

____

____

What do I need to do to achieve my vision?

____

____

____

What do I need to accomplish this year to work toward my vision?

____

____

____

What do I need to do in the next 1 to 5 years to work toward my vision?

____

____

____

What do I need to do in the next 5 to 10 years to work toward my vision?

____

____

____

____

Using Your Vision to Set Goals

Once you have a vision, you need to plan a way to achieve it. That's where goals come in. You will set many goals on your way through this book, just as those who spoke with God had to do. They had to have a goal and take action. In Genesis, God established a new covenant with Noah. God came to Noah and gave him this vision, but in order to achieve it, Noah's first goal was to build the ark. He had to cut the wood to the specifications given by God, he had to build the ark, and he had to fill it with pairs of all of the animals. He and his family had to endure 150 days of flooding, but in the end, God established a new covenant with Noah.

What goals can you set to help you achieve your vision? Be specific. The more specific your goals, the better your execution will be. Get into the details like God did when he gave Noah the exact measurements of the ark. Your goals should lay out as much of the plan as possible.

Goal Setting to Accomplish Your Life Vision

The following categories can help you prioritize certain areas of your life and determine their value in relation to one another. Assign each category a 1, 2, or 3 for you or your family. Mark categories as a 1 if they are the *most important* categories, as a 2 if they are *important but not most important*, and as a 3 if they are *least important*.

Remember: 1's = most important; 2's = important; & 3's = least important

_____Religion
_____Education
_____Saving Money
_____Transportation
_____Starting a New Business
_____Paying Off Debts
_____Culture
_____Other ____________
_____Recreation
_____Family Activities
_____Home Furnishings
_____New House
_____Travel
_____Planned Giving
_____Personal Appearance
_____Other ____________

Goal Setting and Family Goals

Here is your chance to get very specific with the goals for you and/or your family. Think about the future: what goals would you and/or your family like to accomplish? These can be divided into *short-term goals, intermediate goals, and long-term goals.* Goals should be the outcome from your vision exercises and your category-setting.

Short-Term Goals

Short-term goals are goals that you want to achieve in 1 year or less. Write down how much you believe achieving each short-term goal is going to cost, and then start saving that amount per month. Record the date you actually reach your goal.

Intermediate Goals

Intermediate goals are goals that you want to achieve in 1 to 5 years. You may not be able to be as specific as you were with your short-term goals, but the more planning you do now, the more likely you are to follow through with your intermediate goals over time.

Long-Term Goals

Long-term goals are goals you want to achieve in 5 or

more years. Again, you may not be able to be very specific, but there is a good reason to write them down anyway.
It is a proven fact that when you write your goals down, they become a part of your inner being, and you are more likely to achieve them.

This is your place to begin. Your first step into a world of finances may be stressful for you right now, but with vision, action, and a relationship with God, you can quickly be on your way to setting your house in order. (See Goal Sheet at end of chapter.)

Yes, you can do it. You might even be able to see your financially successful house already.

CHAPTER REVIEW: YES, I WILL!

List three things you learned from this chapter that you will put into action in your life.

1. ____

When will you do it?

Immediately   Within the month   Within 6 months

Within 1 year   Within 5 years

2. ____

When will you do it?

Immediately   Within the month   Within 6 months

Within 1 year   Within 5 years

3. ____

When will you do it?

Immediately   Within the month   Within 6 months

Within 1 year   Within 5 years

Today is

____

Goal Sheet

Goal	When	Total Cost	Amount Per Month	Completed
Short term (within 1 year)				
Intermediate (1-5 years)				
Long-Term (Over 5 years)				

Chapter 2
Basics of Budgeting

When you hear people talking about money management, you probably think, "I manage my money. I've got a checking account. I've got a savings account. I've got insurance through work." You're managing. Right?

But what about emergencies? That's when the house you think is in order experiences disorder, and you have to start juggling. The check engine light comes on in the car, and your kids have already grown out of the shoes you just bought them! So out come the credit cards, and your "management" turns into stress and crisis. That is not where you should be – with your family's financial needs hanging in midair, unsupported by a real budget.

. . . and a real vision. That's right: vision.

There are three parts to budgeting your family's money: **vision, action, and achievement.**

Vision:
The Most Important Part of a Budget

We talked about vision in Chapter One, but we can't forget it. The Scripture contains many examples of God giving visions to the faithful – from Abram and Samuel to Joseph, Jabez, and Mary. All were given a vision that allowed them to be used by God.

Throughout God's Word, God tells us to be faithful in how we plan our lives.

Proverbs 29:18 says, *"Where there is no vision people perish, but he that keepeth the law, happy is he"* (KJV).

Proverbs 16:9 says, *"A man's heart plans his way, but the Lord directs his steps."*

Jeremiah 29:11 says, *"'For I know the plans I have for you,' declares the Lord, 'plans to prosper you and not to harm you, plans to give you hope and a future'"* (NIV).

Through such Scriptures, God is encouraging you to be specific in how you see your future and to be sure to include Him in those plans. He is there to give you wisdom, and based on that wisdom, He wants you to take action.

All the vision and wisdom in the world do not matter if you don't take action. For example Mary, the mother of Jesus, was blessed by God with vision. God told her that she would give birth to Jesus. But Jesus didn't just appear out of thin air – POOF! She had to carry him for 9 months and go through the pains of labor before her vision came true.

Business speaker Joel Barker says,

"Vision without action is a dream.
Action without vision is simply passing the time.
Action with vision is making a positive difference."

Composer Gian Carlo Menotti once said,

"Hell begins on the day when God grants us a clear vision of all we might have acheived, of all the gifts which we have wasted, of all that we might have done, which we did not do."

Success takes action, and action begins with thinking. Think about where you want to be, think about where you want to go, and think about your plan and the vision that is guiding you. You need a guiding vision because you are taking a journey from a house of stress to a house of order. And it's not an easy journey.

Taking Action

There are seven big benefits to budgeting that you will see as soon as you start doing a budget diligently.

1. Budgeting allows you to know what is going on with your money.

2. Budgeting gives you control of where your money goes. Don't look at a budget like a straitjacket on your money; instead, it's a rein on your money, guiding it to the right places.
3. Budgeting helps you be more organized. A budget opens your eyes to how much money comes in versus how much money goes out.
4. Budgeting allows for communication – especially in marriage. When you budget and account for all of your spending, including often forgotten things like doctor visits, hair cuts, and car maintenance, you and your spouse will be on the same page. That will strengthen your trust in each other and strengthen your relationship as a whole.
5. Budgeting allows you to take advantage of opportunities. When you look at your spending patterns and match those up with seasonal sales for purchases you need, you can hit the jackpot by finding big bargains.
6. Budgeting saves you time. It may not seem like that at first, but an organized budget, helps you manage your household more efficiently.
7. Finally, budgeting helps you find extra money! That's right: money under control means more money in your pocket!

Learn how to use your budget because it does no good if it

isn't used and followed.

Use your budget to "talk to" your money, and talk to it just like my parents talked to me when I was a child – with rules. Tell your money where it needs to go and when it needs to be there. Tell your money to BEHAVE!

Make your budgeting a family event. If everyone in the house understands how the house is being put in order, then they will obey the rules that the budget imposes on their spending habits.

Don't make the budget so complicated that no one understands it. Don't be the person who chases their family around the house asking, "Who spent the penny?!" A budget is supposed to make your life easier, not more difficult.

Two other concepts are essential to the budgeting process: **appreciation** and **depreciation**.

Appreciation is your friend, and a friend of your money. Appreciation happens when things go up in value. You want to buy things today that have historically shown themselves to be worth more tomorrow, such as stocks, bonds, real estate, and mutual funds.

You also want to find appreciation in yourself. You should grow in mind, body, and spirit. You can't stop getting older, but you can live your life better by getting more education, acquiring a trade, exercising, and having a daily quiet time in prayer and mediation. Also, you can help others, which is a form of giving back to God (Matthew 25:34-40). You need to appreciate yourself and appreciate God for the gifts He has given you.

Depreciation, on the other hand, is your enemy. Depreciation happens when things decrease in their usefulness or value over time. This includes equipment around the house, your car, and even your job. Your job depreciates if you don't develop more diverse skills. In other words, don't become obsolete at work! Keep improving yourself!

Other depreciating items in your budget are children. Don't get me wrong! Kids are great, but watch how you spend your money on them. Many people live beyond their means, using credit cards and becoming financially stressed, just so their kids can wear designer clothes that they are going to outgrow very soon. It's crazy! You could be saving money for your child's education, but instead, you want to make sure they wear a particular brand?

It's the difference between depreciating items and appreciating items that often separates the people living beyond their means from those who aren't. According to studies , 70 percent of people are living beyond their means, leaving just 30 percent of people who are living within their means. The goal is to live below your money. If you do that, what's left over can become wealth.

However, none of this is achieved without God, who uses the simplest terms in His Word to help us understand how we can make money work for us. Consider Solomon's story in the Proverbs: *"Go to the ant, you sluggard! Consider her ways and be wise, which having no captain, overseer or ruler, provides her supplies in the summer, and gathers her food in the harvest"* (Proverbs 6:6-8).

God is telling you to be smart, make a plan, and take action.

The 1-2-3 Budgeting Process

When you are dividing up your money during the budgeting process, you'll find that there are items you *have* to pay and others you *need* to pay. What is left over is for the items you'd *like to have*. When you are making a basic budget, divide your categories into fixed items, variable items, and "like-to-haves."

The first items you put in your budget are fixed items. You have to have them, and they usually stay the same every week or month.

These include:

* Your gross pay
* Your deductions

* Your total income
* Your contribution to church
* Your savings
* Childcare
* Housing
* Utilities
* Insurance
* Car payment
* Gas
* Debt, credit cards, and installment loans.

Next on your budget should be your variable items. They may change from week to week or month to month, but they are necessary. These items include

* Food, groceries, and eating out
* Personal care
* Home maintenance
* Car maintenance
* Body maintenance (doctors, dentists, etc.)

When all of these items have a dollar amount assigned to them, you can move to the like-to-haves.

Some people will see these next items as necessities, but when you are getting your house in order, they can be eliminated or delayed. Among the like-to-haves are

* Furniture
* Recreation and entertainment
* Cell phones
* Cable
* Internet
* Gifts
* Alcohol and tobacco
* Education and self-improvement
* Clothing
* Magazines
* Vacations

When you look at the budget forms at the end of this chapter, you will see how each form is divided.

When you have a dollar amount next to your fixed and variable expenses, you can move on to the next step in the budgeting process – handling cash.

The best budgeting method to use when you are working to get your house in order is the envelope-based system. You need to write your budget categories on different envelopes – childcare, electricity, rent, etc. – cash your check, and fill up those envelopes.

The key to the whole scenario is this: if it is not in the

envelopes, you can't spend it. For example, let's say that you make $1,000 a month, and all your envelopes add up to $1,000. If you say, "I want more money to go out with," and you only budgeted $50 to go out with, you can't cheat! If you don't have it in the "going out" envelope, you don't have it, and you aren't going out.

The envelope method is great to use when you are first starting to gain control of your finances by using a budget. Another budgeting method is the bank account method. Using this method, your paycheck goes straight into your savings account. The way we do it at our house is that we divide our expenses into two categories: household bills and other fixed bills.

My account takes care of the fixed bills, so I move money from the savings account into the checking account to pay those bills. My wife uses her account for the household expenses since she is a good household manager. Whatever is left after she takes care of the household expenses is hers! This gets her in the habit of saving money, which is the best habit you can have.

If you get to the point where saving, investing, and purchasing appreciating items is a habit, you are going to live a life where everything around you goes up in value.
This is where you learn to achieve.

Yes, I Can!

CHAPTER REVIEW: YES, I WILL!

List three things you learned from this chapter that you will put into action in your life.

1. ____

When will you do it?

Immediately Within the month Within 6 months

Within 1 year Within 5 years

2. ____

When will you do it?

Immediately Within the month Within 6 months

Within 1 year Within 5 years

3. ____

When will you do it?

Immediately Within the month Within 6 months

Within 1 year Within 5 years

Today is

____

Budgeting Form

Family Budget

		Periodic Expenses	Date Due	Amount: Actual	Amount: Budget
Gross Income	Salary (1)				
	Salary (2)				
	Interest				
	Dividends				
	Rental				
	Other				
	Total Income			0	0
Payroll Deductions	Elective Payroll Deductions				
	Dental Insurance				
	Medical Insurance				
	Long Term Disability				
	Basic Life Insurance				
	Additional Life Insurance				
	Short Term Disability				
	Long Term Disability				
	Flexible Spending Account				
	Additional Deductions				
	Total Deductions			0	0
	Net Income			0	0

Budgeting Form

Family Budget

			Periodic Expenses		Amount	
				Date Due	Actual	Budget
Must Haves	Household	Emergency Fund: Savings & Investments				
		Contributions				
		His Money - (Daily lunches, etc.)				
		Her Money - (Daily lunches, etc.)				
		Childcare				
		Food and Groceries				
		Food and Groceries -- Meals Eaten Out				
		Personal Care -- Hair Care				
		Personal Care -- Laundry/Dry Cleaning				
	Household Bills	Housing (Rent or Mortgage)				
		Household Maintenance and Repairs				
		Utilities -- Electricity				
		Utilities -- Gas or Other Fuel				
		Utilities -- Water and Sewage				
		Utilities -- Telephone				
		Utilities -- Garbage				
		Insurance -- Property				
		Insurance -- Home				
		Insurance -- Medical				
		Insurance -- Disability				
		Insurance -- Other				
		Business Expenses				
		Taxes	Income			
			Property			
Need to Haves	Secured Debt	Transportation -- Payments (**Don't need**)				
		Transportation -- Gas				
		Transportation -- Bus, Taxi				
		Insurance -- Automobile				
		Automobile	Tags			
			Inspection			
			Maintenance (Oil, Tune-up, Filters, etc.)			

Budgeting Form

Family Budget

			Periodic Expenses		Amount	
				Date Due	Actual	Budget
Like to Haves	Unsecured Debt	Medical -- Doctor				
		Medical -- Dentist				
		Medical -- Drugs				
		Medical -- Others				
		Medical Checkups	Medical			
			Dental			
			Other			
		Monthly Installments -- Department Stores				
		Monthly Installments -- Bank Charge Cards				
		Monthly Installments -- Oil Companies				
		Monthly Installments -- Loans				
		Monthly Installments -- Other				
	After Household items and Debts are Paid	Personal care -- Spa or Health Club				
		Home Furnishings and Equipment				
		Household Help				
		Recreation or Entertainment				
		Recreation or Entertainment -- Cable TV				
		Gifts				
		Education or Self-improvement				
		Food and Groceries -- Alcohol and Tobacco				
		Clothing				
		Gifts	Christmas			
			Birthdays			
			Other			
		Organizational Dues				
		School	Tuition			
			Supplies			
			Books			
		Subscriptions	Magazines			
			CD and Book Clubs			
		Vacations				
		Miscellaneous				
		Total of Income and Expenses			0	0

Chapter 3
Credit: The Good, The Bad and The Ugly

There's nothing that brings more stress to the minds of already financially stressed people than the issue of credit. Credit can bless you or curse you, but when you are working to put your house in order and take control of your money, one of the worse things credit can do is confuse you.

That's why we need to work through the list of credit myths. If you believe them, you will quickly find yourself buried in debt, with your finances out of control.

Myth 1: Financial institutions are there to help you.

WRONG! They are there to make a profit, pure and simple.

Myth 2: You need to use credit cards in order to get the things you want to buy right now.

WRONG! For one thing, you should be saving for big purchases. If you only want a credit card so you can get something right away, you are looking at your wants and not at your needs.

Myth 3: Your financial institution will not give you a spending limit that is too high for you.

WRONG! The lender isn't interested in you but the money that you can pay them. The higher your limit, the more money you owe them.

Myth 4: Your credit card account is your money.

WRONG! That money belongs to the lender. You are just borrowing it. The financial institution reminds you of this every month when you get a bill.

Myth 5: It is not important to understand the terms of your account.

WRONG! All that fine print in your statement really means something, and most of it explains why the lender has an advantage over you. They can raise your limit and your fees whenever they want.

Myth 6: It is for your benefit when your financial institution raises your credit limit.

WRONG! I have heard people that say, "Thank you, Jesus. I didn't know what I was going to do for money. The lender has raised my limit, and I'm better now!" No, you are not. You are *worse* because raising your limit gives you the ability to be in more debt.

Myth 7: You need credit cards to live comfortably.

WRONG! If you need credit cards to live comfortably, you are living beyond your means. Credit cards are part of the problem, not part of the solution.

Myth 8: Using credit cards make life easier.

WRONG! How many people have you heard say, "You've got to have a credit card so you can rent a car!" If that's the only reason people have them, then there are a lot of cars being rented in this country - A LOT! If you think this way, you will be caught in the trap. First, carrying a credit card balance is a convenience for you, then it becomes an obligation, and then it's around for so long you could call it "Junior."

Myth 9: You can have extra money by having more credit cards.

WRONG! You don't have more money; you have the ability to accumulate more debt.

Myth 10: You can control your debt no matter how great it is.

WRONG! This is the biggest myth of all. Sooner or later, that debt will control you.

When it comes down to it, our struggle with the myths of debt speaks to our struggle with true obedience to God. If we want to be blessed by God, we need to listen to His Word and obey because it is in true obedience that we find blessing.

Look at what God says in Deuteronomy about the blessings that come to those who obey and the curses that come on those who don't.

First, the blessings:

"Now it shall come to pass, if you diligently obey the voice of the Lord your God, to observe carefully all His commandments which I command you today, that the Lord your God will set you high above all the nations of the earth. And all these blessings shall come upon you and overtake you, because you obey the voice of the Lord your God... The Lord will open to you his good treasures, the heavens, to give the rain to your land in its season and to bless all the work of your hand. You shall lend to many nations, but you shall not borrow. And the Lord will make you the head and not the tail; you shall be above only, and not be beneath, if you heed the commandments of the Lord your God, which I command you today, and are careful to observe them" (Deuteronomy 28:1-2, 12-13).

What about the people who don't obey?

"But it shall come to pass, if you do not obey the voice of the Lord your God, to observe carefully all His commandments and His statutes which I command you today, that all these curses will come upon you and overtake you: ...The alien who is among you shall rise higher and higher above you, and you shall come down lower and lower. He shall lend to you, but you shall not lend to

him; he shall be the head and you shall be the tail. Moreover all these curses shall come upon you and pursue and overtake you, until you are destroyed, because you did not obey the voice of the Lord your God, to keep His commandments and his statutes which He commanded you" (Deuteronomy 28:15, 43-45).

Notice that the Word is very direct when it talks about borrowing. Those who lend but don't borrow are to be blessed. God does not want you to be confused about money; that is why He has blessed you with instructions to keep you out of trouble.

Remember what He says in Proverbs: *"The rich rules over the poor, and the borrower is slave to the lender"* (Proverbs 22:7).

Right now, we are killing ourselves with debt, handcuffing ourselves from being able to do the right thing. God asks us to feed the hungry, and we aren't able to do that because of our debt.

We can't be used by God because we are too busy trying to pay the Devil!

To put it in perspective, look at the number of hours you work in order to get something. Do you know that to buy a $30,000 car, someone making $10 an hour has to work for a year and a half to pay for the car? And that's just the car! All of those other bills have to be paid somehow.

Credit equals debt. Do not make the mistake of thinking

that credit is a good thing. You are buying now and paying more later. When you do that, you create debt.

Credit is a tool and can be used for good purposes but not when it is used for the wrong purposes. If you are using credit to live beyond your means, then you are using it for the wrong reason.

The Different Types of Credit

You will encounter several different types of credit in your financial life.

The first is service: you have services rendered and then pay for them later. An example of service debt is credit from a doctor or dentist with no interest being charged.

The second is utilities: you get utilities in your home and pay for them later.

The third is secured credit: an installment plan is "secured" by items you buy, like a home, a car, or furniture.

Next is unsecured credit: it is a line of credit that you can use to pay for something you want. Credit cards fall into this category.

Finally there are personal loans, which can be secured or unsecured. Payday loans and check-cashing loans are secured because the lender has access to your checking account when you leave a post-dated check.

But let's be clear: those places cost you money. You need to understand the cost of high credit and the ways that the fees can add up. For example, I counseled a woman who used a payday loan business and repeatedly rolled over her fees. Eventually, she paid about $4,000 on the $600 she initially borrowed. To avoid a situation like this, when you get any sort of credit, you have to clearly understand the terms and ask questions like, "What is the amount of the loan? What is the interest rate (which helps you figure the finance charge)? What is the length of time it will take to repay the loan? Could I save up the money in a shorter period of time and pay cash?" These are the questions you must answer when you are struggling to get out of the handcuffs of debt.

The Good of Debt

Now we are going to discuss the good, the bad, and the ugly of debt. While it's best to get rid of all the debt that you can and secure yourself with your own emergency fund, there can be some benefits of debt.

* Use it to buy large, appreciating goods and services. The best example is a home.
* Use it to deal with emergencies that exceed your emergency fund. (You should have at least 3 to 6 months

of living expenses in your emergency fund.)

* Use it to take advantage of opportunities. You have to be very careful with this. You want to take advantage of a great deal, but you don't want to make a habit of using credit to do it.
* Use it for convenience but always within limits.
* Use it to establish or improve your credit rating. Do note, however, that this can be done without credit cards by paying your utilities and any other bill on time and in full.

The Bad of Debt

* The price of debt is just too high. Not only do you get in over your head when you buy something you can't afford, but you are also hit by interest, fees, late fees, over-the-limit fees, and penalties. They all add up very, very fast.
* There is also the potential of liability. Most creditors limit your liability to $50 when fraud is involved with your card. However, if you don't detect fraud on your card over a certain number of days, then you are liable for the entire fraudulent amount. Someone can charge $5,000 on your card, and if you don't notice it in time, you will owe the entire $5,000.
* Also consider the issue of endangered privacy. The more

information about yourself that is out there, the bigger chance of your identity being compromised!

Take a long look at how much your debts take from your total income. How do these debts make you feel? This is where stress can get out of control and send you into a financial tailspin.

Any debt that takes 10% or less of your income is OK. Debt that takes 16 to 20 percent of your income means you are totally extended. When debt payments total 26 percent or more of your income, you are in a **financial disaster.**

The Ugly of Debt

* You are tempted to overspend.
* Your interest rates can skyrocket.
* You are living beyond your means.
* You have a loss of freedom.

Between 150 and 200 million credit cards have been issued annually since 2000, adding up to 1.2 billion credit cards in current circulation. Who makes money from your credit card debt? The companies that issue the cards. 2003 was a bad year for the economy, but in that same year, credit card issuers made $20 *billion* in profit. They are really quiet about their profits. If the world knew they made $20 billion dollars profit each year, people would think twice about charging. Using credit has put our country in the mess that it's in.

Action Plan to Get Out of Debt

Again, go back to your vision that we talked about in the first chapter. What is the vision for your life? What are your family's financial goals? Revisiting those questions should be the first step in taking action to get out of debt.

Here are some other actions that will help you get out of debt and put your house in order:

* Budget and track your expenses, which was covered in Chapter 2.
* Inventory your credit. Take stock of all the debts you have, how much of your income you are spending on them, and when they are due. (See Debt Reduction Kit 2 at end of this chapter.)
* Cut up your credit cards. If you want to reach your vision, you won't need them any more.
* Pay off the balances. Pay them off in order from smallest to largest. When you pay off the first debt, roll that payment amount into paying off the next smallest debt until all your debts are paid off. That's called a debt snowball.

* After the balances are paid, send a certified letter to your creditors requesting them to close your account and to note that the account was "closed at account owner's request."
* Opt-out of pre-approved offers.
* Check and clean up your credit.

This last point is very important. Your credit score is important, so you need to be able to manage your score while you are in your debt elimination program.

What is a Credit Score?

Everyone keeps score - not just on the playground or the football field but in the real world of finances as well. Credit scoring is the process of evaluating credit accounts and payment history data for an individual in order to score that person's credit-worthiness. Credit scoring helps lenders and other groups make certain types of decisions:

* Lending decisions: Decisions regarding whether to grant credit or not.
* Servicing decisions: Decisions regarding who will need their payments postponed because they are not made on time.
* Collection decisions: Decisions regarding who is most

likely to default on a credit agreement.

* Marketing decisions: Decisions regarding who will get pre-approved offers of credit.
* Business decisions: Decisions regarding how much risk a customer presents.

Credit scoring converts large amounts of difficult-to-compare data into a single point score for comparison. In the world of credit, the higher your credit score, the lower the rate at which you can borrow money.

Three Things You Need in Order to Have a Credit Score

1. One credit relationship with a business that is tracked on your credit report for at least 6 months or updated at a credit reporting agency within the last 6 months.
2. A legitimate Social Security Number.
3. Not being on the Office of Foreign Asset Control (OFAC) list. OFAC enforces economic and trade sanctions against countries and groups of individuals involved in terrorism, narcotics, and other disreputable activities.

A credit score is not a perfect measurement of your credit

management skills; it is the way lenders measure you. You may encounter problems when you or a business checks out your credit score, problems such as incomplete information, inaccurate information, or identity theft.

The three primary collectors of payment history data are Experian, TransUnion, and Equifax. Creditors contract with these bureaus and send them data, which are analyzed to determine payment patterns. These patterns help predict the likelihood that people will make future payments on time.

A credit score is a numeric representation of how likely you are to be 90 days late paying any of your creditors over the next 24 months. Credit scores range from 150 to 990. Any score above 650 is considered very good. You credit score will focus on your last 24 months of activity.

Ways to Manage Your Credit Score When Eliminating Your Debt

* Pay your debts on time. Do not concentrate on one debt so intensely that you fail to pay another debt. A consistent record of on-time payments will help your credit score.
* Check your credit report regularly. If you find an inaccuracy or incomplete item on your credit report, contact the creditor or the credit bureau to fix it promptly.

* Remember: a low credit score cannot be fixed overnight! Your credit score will improve as your overall credit improves, and this process takes time.
* Make sure that all your creditors are reporting the correct credit limit on your credit reports. You can increase your credit score if your revolving account balances are below 30% of their High Credit Limit.
* Do not close accounts until you are completely free of all credit card debts. Stop using the credit accounts; just don't close them yet. Closing accounts that have been opened the longest (well-seasoned) should be the last thing that you do. Having well-seasoned accounts are an important part of your credit history.
* Get credit counseling if you feel it is necessary. However, do not implement any type of debt repayment plan (erasing part of your debt) with your creditors, such as filing Chapter 13 bankruptcy or negotiating a lower balance for your existing debts. Repayment plans can wreak havoc on your credit file.
* Say "NO!" to any new credit.
* Don't file bankruptcy or get foreclosed on. Work with your creditors to reconcile and repay your accounts. Did you know that you can ask lenders (especially credit card agencies) to lower your interest rate or adjust the

required minimum payment? Call your lenders and ask, and keep the lines of communication open with them. Most importantly, do not try to decide on the best course of action without praying and seeking a wise Christian counselor.

* If you plan to buy a home, check your credit report 6 months before starting the process. Do not wait until the last minute to check it.

If you ever get in a pinch and need to correct your credit file quickly, there is a way to delete credit report errors in 48 hours. This is the absolute fastest way to correct errors on your credit report and raise your credit score. However, it can only be done through a mortgage company or a bank. If you apply for a home loan and find errors on your credit report, ask the loan officer to conduct a Rapid Rescore. Rapid Rescore is a service offered by the credit bureaus for quickly correcting erroneous information in a credit file. Don't mistake this for the credit clinic tactic of multiple dispute letters. The Rapid Rescore strategy requires proper paperwork. You need proof that comes directly from the creditor, showing that the item is incorrect. For example, such proof could include a letter stating that an account is not yours, a letter stating the account was paid satisfactorily, a release of lien, a satisfaction of judgment, a bankruptcy discharge, a letter for deletion of collection account, or any relevant evidence. The results are not guaranteed and will cost you about $50 per account per credit reporting agency.

Please don't mistake this chapter as advocating debt. You should be honest with your practices in paying off your debt and clearing up your credit score.

During my years of helping people with their credit, I found people lowered their credit scores while trying to eliminate their debt before they fully understood the credit scoring process.

Always . . . .

Pray for God's directions before starting your debt elimination plan.

Pray for God to keep your vision clear as you go through all of these steps.

Pray for God to give you action and to help you put your house in order!

Yes, You Can Set Your House in Order!

CHAPTER REVIEW: YES, I WILL!

List three things you learned from this chapter that you will put into action in your life.

1. ____

When will you do it?

Immediately   Within the month   Within 6 months

Within 1 year   Within 5 years

2. ____

When will you do it?

Immediately   Within the month   Within 6 months

Within 1 year   Within 5 years

3. ____

When will you do it?

Immediately   Within the month   Within 6 months

Within 1 year   Within 5 years

Today is

____

Debt Reduction Kit 1

Use the following information in order to get out of debt. The information within this kit is not meant to be all-encompassing regarding your debt but can help you become debt free.

1. Determine the vision for your life.

____

____

____

____

2. Establish goals and a budget to track and plan your expenses.
3. Inventory your credit.
4. Cut up your credit cards.
5. Pay off the balances (Snowball method, Debt Accelerator, etc.).
6. After the balances are paid, send a certified letter to your creditors requesting them to close your account and to specifically note on the account "Closed at account owner's request."
7. Opt out of pre-approved offers.
8. Check and clean-up your credit report.

Debt Reduction Kit 2

Step 1 – Determine to be debt-free.
Step 2 – Count up the costs of debt.
Step 3 – Determine the payoff order.
Step 4 – Pay off your debts and become debt-free.

(2)Name of Card/Loan	(3) Payoff Order	(2) Owed	(2) Int. Rate	(2)Monthly Pymt
1.				
2.				
3.				
4.				
5.				
6.				
7.				
8.				
9.				
10.				
11.				
12.				

Things to do:

• Cut up your credit cards, and think before buying anything on credit.

• Ask creditors to reduce your interest rate (If you have been frequently late in making payments or are deep in debt, this may not be possible.).

• Pay off one debt at a time.

• Once a debt is paid off, apply the payment from the previous debt toward the next debt.

• Remember that it took time to get in debt, and it will take time to get out of debt.

• Do not use debt consolidation until your spending problem is cured. Debt consolidation does not eliminate debt; it merely juggles it around.

Debt Reduction Kit 3

Letters to Credit Company and Credit Reporting Agency
Sample letter #1 Closing a credit account

Date
Your Name
Your Address
Your City, State, Zip Code

Customer Service Department
Name of Credit Company
Address
City, State, Zip Code

Dear Sir or Madam:
I would like to cancel my account, # (fill in the account number). I request that you close this account immediately. Upon closing the account, please report to the credit bureaus that the account was "closed at request of cardholder," and mail me a confirmation upon completion.

Sincerely,
Your name

Sample letter #2 – Disputing errors on your credit history
Date
Your Name
Your Address
Your City, State, Zip Code

Complaint Department
Name of Credit Reporting Agency
Address
City, State, Zip Code

Dear Sir or Madam:
I am writing to dispute the following information in my file. The items I dispute are also encircled on the attached copy of the report I received. (Identify item(s) disputed by name of source, such as creditors or tax court, and identify type of item, such as credit account, judgment, etc.) This item is (inaccurate or incomplete) because (describe what is inaccurate or incomplete and why). I am requesting that the item be deleted (or request another specific change) to correct the information.

Enclosed are copies of (use this sentence if applicable and describe any enclosed documentation, such as payment records, court documents, etc.), supporting my position. Please reinvestigate this (these) matter(s) and (delete or correct) the disputed item(s) as soon as possible.

Sincerely,
Your name
Enclosures: (List what you are enclosing)

Debt Reduction Kit 4

Stop unsolicited pre-approved offers of credit or insurance

Every day your mailbox may contain an interesting offer of pre-approved credit or insurance. These offers give you numerous choices and opportunities. However, while millions of Americans welcome these choices, others prefer not to receive such offers.

Your rights as a consumer include the ability to "opt-out," which prevents consumer credit reporting companies from using your credit file information for pre-approved offers of credit or insurance. The consumer credit reporting companies, Equifax, Experian, Innovis, and TransUnion, want to help companies give American consumers the choices they want, including the right to say, "Please don't send me these offers." That's why the four consumer credit reporting companies have developed www.optoutprescreen.com . Please note: this process may not be used to opt-out businesses or companies.

If you want to remove your name from lists for pre-approved offers of credit or insurance obtained from these four consumer credit reporting companies, you will need to provide your personal information using one of the methods below. Once you provide your information, your name will be removed from eligibility for pre-approved offer lists provided by all four companies. The information you provide is confidential and will only be used to process your request.

You may request to opt-out from pre-approved offer lists for 5 years or permanently. If you have previously completed a request to opt-out and would like to opt-in, you may also complete your request using the web-site method. Even though your request via the web method becomes effective with Equifax, Experian, Innovis, and TransUnion within 5 days of your request, you may not see an immediate reduction in the number of offers you receive because your name may have already been provided to some companies which have not yet mailed their offers to you. Removing your name from these pre-approved lists does not affect your ability to apply for or obtain credit or insurance.

If you opt-out, you will simply not be included in pre-approved offer lists obtained from these four consumer credit reporting companies. However, you may continue to receive commercial mailings based on lists from other sources.

Mail (download form from Federal Trade Commission web site):
http://www.ftc.gov/privacy/cred ltr.htm
Web: *WWW.OPTOUTPRESCREEN.COM*

Telephone:
You can make one phone call to 1-888-567-8688 [1-888-5-OPTOUT] to opt-out of all pre-screened offers. After the language option, you can choose one of the following:
Select Option 1 – exclude your name for 5 years
Select Option 2 – include your name
Select Option 3 – exclude your name permanently

The Direct Marketing Association (DMA) also tracks consumers who prefer not to receive mail or telephone solicitations. The DMA can provide information about opting out of lists produced by companies that subscribe to its mail and telephone preference services. You may contact the DMA at the following web address: *http://www.dmaconsumers.org/consumerassistance.html.*
Opting out will not end solicitations from all local merchants, religious and charitable associations, professional and alumni associations, politicians, and companies with which you conduct business. To eliminate mail from these groups - as well as mail addressed to "occupant" or "resident" - write directly to each source.

Chapter 4
Making Every Penny Work Hard

Once you get serious about budgeting, should you really worry about every penny that passes through your hand? Yes! Just think about it: if you make $25,000 a year between the ages of 20 and 67, $1 million dollars will pass through your hands. The problem is that, without a budget, you will have spent a million dollars and probably won't know where it all went!

Changing just a little bit of the formula – such as living on $23,000 instead of $25,000 – can make a tremendous difference. That's $94,000 that you get to keep - and that's not including any growth with the money! Finding pennies is the difference between saving your raise when you get it and spending it on something you don't need – and being worse off!

You already know about the vision, knowledge, and action it takes to get you from a financial mess to life on a disciplined budget, but dark clouds can still roll in. The biggest is an unexpected financial emergency, which can take people with no budget and throw them into a tailspin.

Emergency is depreciation's brother. It makes you stress and worry about the razor-thin margin you have between getting by and falling into chaos. It can be a car breaking down, a hospital stay, or the wear and tear caused by all of those depreciating items around your home.

Everything will break and will need to be replaced. What you need to do is be prepared and use your budget to PLAN for emergencies.

When you have an emergency and no budget, everything is urgent. When you have an emergency and a good budget, everything is expected. For example, I knew those tires would need replacing, and I've been saving up for them!

Emergencies are normal. So how do you prepare for them? Make sure that funding for emergencies is a vital part of your budget.

The Budget Rule:

The ideal family budget formula is <u>your income = your savings/emergency fund + your expenses.</u>

Go back to your budgeting forms and make sure you have money set aside for savings and emergencies. Squeeze every penny you can to get the money you need in there. Have an envelope set aside for emergencies or a savings account for them, depending on which method you use.

The two keys to maintaining a great budget are managing your expenses and tracking them. One of the ways we help people set their house in order is by having them write down all of their expenses for a short period of time. This helps them see just how much they are really spending on things like lunch and coffee.

You want to maximize your income, and you do that by making your money work as hard as you do.

Maximizing Your Income

You were meant to work, and it wasn't meant to be easy. Giving your work anything less than your best effort goes against what is written in the Scripture. The first worker was Adam. Genesis 2:15 says, *"The Lord God took the man and put him in the Garden of Eden to tend and to keep it,"* establishing the first job. In Ecclesiastes 9:10, the Word says work was meant to be done with full effort: *"Whatever your hand finds to do, do it with your might for there is no work or device or knowledge or wisdom in the grave where you are going."*

It may be a little discouraging sometimes to see just where all of that hard-earned money goes. When you get your paycheck, you see all the money that has been taken out of it for taxes and deductions. But remember, Christ told us to "....*render to Caesar the things that are Caesar's, and to God the things that are God's*" (Mark 12:17), so you should understand that you will have very little control over parts of your paycheck. You can't directly control your hours, your earnings, or your taxes, but you can control the pre-tax and after-tax deductions.

When you are looking to get the biggest bang for your buck, you need to examine all of your deductions, especially the pre-tax items. These serve an extra special purpose because they benefit you through insurance and retirement coverage by lowering the income you have to pay taxes on.

Some pre-tax items are medical insurance, a retirement plan (which can also have a match from employers – free money!), and a flexible spending account (FSA). FSAs allow you to set aside money for medical and childcare expenses that would otherwise come out of your pocket.

If you don't take advantage of pre-tax deductions, you are missing out on a great deal. The more pre-tax deductions you have, the lower your total taxes will be.

After-tax deductions offer no immediate tax benefit but do include important pieces of your financial picture that you will want to contribute to, including disability and long-term insurance and retirement plans. One retirement plan to look into is an Individual Retirement Account (IRA). IRAs come from after-tax deductions when you contribute to them, but they can save you taxes when you withdraw your money at retirement or at tax time.

Will all that money add up? Yes, it will! YES, IT WILL!

Why? Because of the miracle of compound interest. Einstein called compound interest the eighth wonder of the world. It's the way money grows over a long period of time as it multiples itself. You will be amazed how quickly a $30 contribution each month to an IRA can grow when earning 12 percent interest. How much could it earn over 20 years? $104,849! That's after contributing only $10,800 of your own money. Wow!

This is why when you make a budget you need to have your long-term goals – your vision – always in mind. Do you want to budget $30 a month for coffee when you could be accumulating more than $100,000 in 20 years?

If you have the vision, action, and discipline that come with good budgeting, then you can take time to celebrate your accomplishments with the Lord.

Go ahead and have a party. You have seen what God can do for you and what He can bring to your life.

As it says in Job 36:11-12, *"If they obey and serve Him, they shall spend their days in prosperity, and their years in pleasures. But if they do not obey, they shall perish by the sword, and they shall die without knowledge."*

CHAPTER REVIEW: YES, I WILL!

List three things you learned from this chapter that you will put into action in your life.

1. ____

When will you do it?

Immediately Within the month Within 6 months

Within 1 year Within 5 years

2. ____

When will you do it?

Immediately Within the month Within 6 months

Within 1 year Within 5 years

3. ____

When will you do it?

Immediately Within the month Within 6 months

Within 1 year Within 5 years

Today is

____

Chapter 5
Your Relationship With God And Money

Look around your home at all of the things you have: a television, refrigerator, a car and a closet full of clothes.

And you aren't done shopping for material goods, are you? You probably bought some more things just this week.

Now let's think about what God thinks of all those things.

Jesus said in Luke 9:58, *"Foxes have holes and birds of the air have nests, but the Son of Man has nowhere to lay his head."*

When it came to material goods, Christ Himself had none. He had no home. He had only the clothes on his back. He relied not on a job but on God's grace and those around him.

To Jesus, possessions had no meaning.

So it should be for us. Our relationship with God should be valued above all things, especially those things that are valued here on Earth.

As we put our financial house in order, we rest it on the foundation of our income. But that does not mean we put income above all things. Instead, we place it there because we are overseeing our income for God.

All of our possessions and money belong to God, but it is up to us to manage them well for Him while we are on Earth.

That is why we need to take the will of God and the glorification of His kingdom into account with every financial move we make.

When you buy something, always ask yourself this question: What is that purchase doing to glorify God? Perhaps it is strengthening your relationship with your family. Or maybe it is distancing yourself from your family. When you're buying dinner, it may be for the nourishment of your body. Or, if it's junk food, it could be the opposite. How your finances impact your relationship with God should be at the forefront of your mind for every decision you make.

This brings us to tithing. Tithing is fundamental to a Christian. Tithing is not strictly Old Testament or New Testament theory. Tithing is quite simply giving back to God that which He has most graciously allowed you to have.

If you have the proper relationship with God, all that you have is not too much to give to Him. It is all His to begin with.

Remember the attributes of God listed in Chapter One? Among the greatest attributes of God is His unchanging nature. God existed in the beginning, exists now, and will exist in the future. He comes to the discontented, wherever they might be. He knows where you are and what your needs are.

God will meet your needs, just as He met the needs of Christ on Earth and just as Christ said He takes care of the animals in nature as well.

All you need to do is listen to God and ask Him how you can give Him glory while you are on Earth.

Of course, that's the point, isn't it?

Look around your home again. All of those material goods are fleeting, as is your time on Earth. You will die, and if you have accepted Christ, you will spend eternity in Heaven, where the unimportance of material goods will truly come into perspective.

In Heaven, where the roads are golden and the gates are made of pearls, no one will care about material splendor. In Heaven, no one is trying to pluck a pearl from the gate. No one is scraping the gold off the roads.

When you are in the presence of God, none of that wealth will matter.

Give God the glory on Earth with every financial move you make, and you will find glory with him in Heaven if you are His child.

CHAPTER REVIEW: YES, I WILL!

List three things you learned from this chapter that you will put into action in your life.

1. ____

When will you do it?

Immediately   Within the month   Within 6 months

Within 1 year   Within 5 years

2. ____

When will you do it?

Immediately   Within the month   Within 6 months

Within 1 year   Within 5 years

3. ____

When will you do it?

Immediately   Within the month   Within 6 months

Within 1 year   Within 5 years

Today is

____

Chapter 6
Drive Right: Transportation

Everyone wants a nice car, right?

If you get one that's really nice, you don't even want to put it in your garage! You want to display it in front of your house so everyone can see it! Or you want to drive around town, with your car all washed and polished so the guy in the lane next to you can check you out!

But would you be surprised to know that some of the most financially successful people in the country aren't concerned at all with flashy cars. In fact, they do their best to minimize expenses related to transportation because these expenses take away from their wealth.

As we begin to look at transportation and car expenses, we should look at what God says about material goods and at what wealthy people have to say about where their money goes in the area of transportation.

The lesson we need to remember from Scripture is that we should use material goods to do God's will. My money belongs to Him, my house belongs to Him, and my car belongs to Him.

Buying a car isn't for your ego. It isn't for showing off your status. It is to get you where you are going on your road to glorifying God.

Proverbs 21:17 says, *"He who loves pleasure will become a poor man; He who loves wine and oil will not become rich."*

In their book *The Millionaire Next Door*, Thomas Stanley and William Danko studied the characteristics of millionaires and looked at what they had in common and how they kept themselves wealthy. They found that most of them kept this Biblical principle. They did not buy things for pleasure but used their wealth wisely.

"The foundation stone of wealth accumulation is defense and this defense should be anchored by budgeting and planning," the book says.

When it came to buying something like a car, the millionaires believed in living well below their means. They believed that financial independence was more important than displaying high social status, and they were proficient in targeting market opportunities.

How can you use all of that advice, as well as the Word of

God, to make a difference in the transportation you buy? Simply by following the ABC's of minimizing transportation expenses.

ABC's to Getting Into the Right (and Right-Priced) Car

There are three key points when it comes to getting a car:

A. Always have a Budget

When you are working to get your house in order, you are always going to consult your budget when it comes to major purchases. Besides your home, a car is going to be one of the most expensive items you buy.

What does your budget say about buying a vehicle? How much can you really afford to pay?

The cornerstone to finding out what you can afford is determining your debt payment limit as a percent of your income. If your debt payments take up 10 percent or less of your total income, then you are not under pressure of debt, but as that percentage increases, you are moving closer and closer to a debt disaster.

Take all of your bills and figure out what your debt percentage is. If you add a car payment to your bills, what does your debt percentage go up to? Having a budget makes discovering this amount easier.

I cannot emphasize this enough: You cannot get by without having a written budget! Living by a budget is like flossing your teeth. If the upkeep is diligent, in the end, you'll have a great smile, and your teeth will last a long time. Not living on a budget is like eating a lot of sugar. It may taste good at the time, but afterward, you'll have cavities and teeth that look GROSS!

Remember the purpose of your budget:

1. Getting out of debt
2. Planning in advance
3. Knowing where your money is going
4. Maximizing the power of your money.

How does a car fit into this? No matter what kind of car you get, it is going to be a drain on your budget because it is a depreciating item.

Remember, you want more historically appreciating items in your finances, like a home – something you buy today that's worth more tomorrow. Depreciating items are things you buy today that are worth less tomorrow.

To keep depreciation from hurting you, buy your

transportation in the best possible way: pay with cash. If you can't save up and pay cash for a car, you need to look at a 3-year payoff plan, which is the next best option.

In order to hit a home run with that 3-year payoff you need to know three things: 1) the price you can afford (be honest with yourself and your budget); 2) the highest down payment you can make (the higher the better), and 3) the monthly payment can you afford after looking at your debt percentage.

Remember again what God's Word says about material goods: You need to set your wants and your ego aside for your real needs. If all you need is a car to get you from Point A to Point B, then you don't need to purchase the most expensive vehicle on the lot.

A used car, which is 3 years old or older, is always a better option than a new car. You will save on the overall cost, all of the costs that come with ownership (tags, title, insurance, etc.), as well as the depreciation.

Remember, your car is depreciating as soon as you sign your temporary title, and you want your money to grow, not evaporate.

B. Be Diligent in Research

You need to be an informed buyer before you buy a vehicle. This can't be a rash decision or impulse purchase. Thankfully, there are many places where you can find the fair price to pay for your transportation.

Start at the library and read the *NADA* (National Automobile Dealers Association) Guide or the *Kelley Blue Book*. You can also look at Consumer Reports, which creates a guide every April that is very informative, and you can check out the internet for comments by people who purchased a similar vehicle.

C. Negotiate

People often say that a sharp car salesman is like a shark. If you don't follow points A, B, and C, not only are you diving into the water with the sharks, not knowing how to swim, but you are diving in with cuts all over your body.

There is blood in the water! LOOK OUT! THE SHARKS WILL EAT YOU UP!

Your wealth will diminish if you don't have a good position from which to negotiate.

When it comes to buying a car, there are six different types of car buyers:

1. **The cash buyer:** This person has cash in hand to purchase the car.
2. **The difference buyer:** This person wants to haggle between price differences in order to get the best deal.
3. **The allowance buyer:** This person saw ads for different allowances (such as $1,500 cash back) and wants to use those to get the best price.
4. **Payment buyers:** This buyer's shopping is based strictly on the payment he or she can squeeze into his or her budget.
5. **Lease buyers:** This buyer is looking for a lease and isn't interested in buying.
6. **The last and best buyer – the cash and informed buyer.** This is the buyer you want to be! You have the money in your hand, and the knowledge in your brain to get the best possible deal. You know your budget, you know the best type of car for you, and you know how much the car should cost.

In order to use your power as a consumer to your advantage, follow these simple negotiating skills: 1) Know what your trade-in is worth. 2) Know what the car you are buying is worth. 3) Shop around.

"Shopping twins" is a good strategy. Find two similar cars so that you aren't locked into one particular model, and then negotiate on both of them. Working two deals at once will allow you to make the best deal possible.

Remember, the purchase price is not the only piece of your negotiation. You also need to negotiate the financing (if you need it) and the amount of your trade-in. You don't want to intermingle these three parts. Always do them separately!

The date and time to purchase a vehicle are important, too. Not all days are created equal. If you go to purchase a vehicle at the end of the month, salesmen are going to be looking to meet their sales goals. Also, July, August and December are traditionally slow months for car sales. Take advantage of the salesman's need for your purchase. Even the day of the week matters. Mondays, Tuesdays, and Thursdays are slow for dealers – and great for you!

Don't let a salesman distract you by focusing on the payment amount. That is how they want to dictate the sale. You want to drive the conversation with your research, your vision, and your budget.

You are buying transportation in a godly way with the understanding that even buying a car can be done for the glory of God.

You want those sharks swimming in the water to be hungry, but you want to be holding the pole instead of being the bait!

You can do it. Yes, You Can!

CHAPTER REVIEW: YES, I WILL!

List three things you learned from this chapter that you will put into action in your life.

1. ____

When will you do it?

Immediately   Within the month   Within 6 months

Within 1 year   Within 5 years

2. ____

When will you do it?

Immediately   Within the month   Within 6 months

Within 1 year   Within 5 years

3. ____

When will you do it?

Immediately   Within the month   Within 6 months

Within 1 year   Within 5 years

Today is

____

Chapter 7
Live Right: Housing

My wife and I thought we had it all when we had a new home filled with new things: a new refrigerator, a new washing machine, and a new dryer. We had new paint on the outside and new carpet on the inside.

It was a designer home, and it was all that we wanted it to be. But along with all this newness came an abundance of new debt.

Not long after, we had to sell that house, put all those new things in storage, and move in with her mother. What had we done wrong? We hadn't followed the Scripture that says, *"Prepare your outside work, Make it fit for yourself in the field; And afterward build your house"* (Proverbs 24:27). We found a house, but we did not do our "outside work."

What is your "outside work"? Your outside work is the finances you need to get in order before you buy a home, including your debt and your credit.

Before you have a house that becomes a home, you

need to make sure you are on solid financial ground!

Eventually, the Lord blessed us with the opportunity to do a paper route, work hard, save up, and get into our next home the right way.

If I had known about Proverbs 24:27 at that time and applied it to my life, we would not have gone through the things that we did. Get it right on the outside, and soon you will move inside your new home.

Renting vs. Owning

Perhaps you are still debating whether buying a home is for you. There are advantages and disadvantages to renting, as well as advantages and disadvantages to buying.

Advantages of Renting

Maintenance

When you rent, you get a lot of peace of mind because you don't have to worry about maintenance. If your roof starts to leak in your rental property, you just call the landlord.

Freedom

It's easy to pick up and move if you are renting. If you don't like your neighbors, you can move. If you find a better deal, you can move.

Equity

You aren't losing equity when you rent.

What is equity? Equity is the difference between what a home is worth versus what you owe on it. If the property loses value, it doesn't affect you financially, just the owner.

Disadvantages of Renting

No Equity

Purchasing a home is considered a great investment, and renting gains you no equity.

No Personalization

You cannot personalize your rented place. I lived with those restrictions for so long. I didn't put anything on the walls of my dorm, and then I moved into an apartment and still could not decorate. It was against the rules!

Inflation

Rent can fluctuate. If inflation goes up, just wait, because your rent will go up, too.

Restrictions

There are lots of restrictions when you are renting. No pets, no noise, and, in some places, no kids!

Ownership

Finally, you don't have pride in ownership when you are renting. What you have looks like what other people have. You aren't able to show your friends something you feel special about.

Advantages of Owning

Equity

Owning a home will most likely increase your net worth. In most cases, homes increase in value due to supply, demand, and availability of homes in a specific price range. There are two ways to increase your equity:
by the value of your home growing through the market or by you paying down the balance you owe on your home through your mortgage payments every month.

Predictable Payments

If you have a house and a standard mortgage, you will have predictable payments.

Stability

Owning a home also gets you stability. It is not going anywhere. You will not wake up one morning and someone tell you that you must move. The property owner has decided to turn their rental properties into a movie theatre. I can drive by the houses that we have owned, and there they still sit. There is a peace-of-mind that comes with that stability.

Tax Advantages

You are able to get a deduction on the interest you pay on your loan that you don't get when you are renting.

Personalization

Finally, you can personalize a home. It doesn't matter how big or small your house is: it's your house, and if you keep it up, it will benefit you. You can even get a dog!

Disadvantages of Owning

Maintenance and Repairs

If something is broken, you have to fix it. Maintenance and repairs are costs that people often overlook. When I was young, everything we needed was always in Dad's shed – an edger, a lawnmower, and all of the other tools. When you are a homeowner, you have to buy all of that yourself! You won't believe how much all of that costs when you are first starting out. It can be thousands, and that doesn't count all those trips to the hardware store for little miscellaneous items.

Unpleasant Neighbors

Problem neighbors can be a huge disadvantage when you own a home. You usually don't learn about them until you've already signed your mortgage. Have the wrong sort of neighbor, and you could quickly end up on one of those TV court shows. Nobody wants that!

Miscellaneous Expenses

There are many financial obligations associated with getting into a house: the down payment (which can be avoided), the cost of moving, the cost of insurance (which can fluctuate), and the cost of property taxes (which will typically only go up). You need to look at more than just the cost of the mortgage payment when you are thinking about buying a home.

Then, there are the initial costs of moving in. Paying deposits on utility bills, paying to have the TV hooked up, renting a moving van or truck, and purchasing cleaning supplies to clean the house even before moving in are just a few…not to mention that you will probably live in the house several days before you cook your first meal because the pots and pans and dishes are still in boxes – so you eat pizza out or bring home burgers. If you own a home that you are leaving, you also need money to fix up that home so it will show properly and sell quickly.

Credit Card Solicitation

Another disadvantage of owning a home is that, as soon as your name is on the closing statement, banks will start sending you pre-approval letters for credit cards because your credit rating (not necessarily score) will sky rocket - not to mention your own personal self-esteem. Be careful when you purchase your new home. Pride comes before destruction.

My Finances

When it comes to deciding whether you are going to rent or buy, you need to rely on more than just your calculator. In some instances, a home will cost more than a similar sized rental, and in others, it will cost less. You need to look at the facts and not let your family, a lender, or a real estate agent make that decision for you. Again, refer to Scripture. In Luke, the Lord Jesus talks about looking at the financial facts before making a big decision.

"For which of you, intending to build a tower, does not sit down first and count the cost, whether he has enough to finish it? Lest, after he has laid the foundation, and is not able to finish, all who see it begin to mock him, saying 'This man began to build and was not able to finish'" (Luke 14:28-30).

You will make the right decision if you examine your finances and count the costs before making any decision.

Your Budget

You may be so excited about the prospect of owning a home that you want to dive right in and buy a house, regardless of what your budget looks like.

NEVER DO THAT!

Without a budget, you are like a ship with no rudder, a bike with no handle bars, a train without a track: totally out of control. You *must* have a budget first. A budget is your financial guide to living below your means and becoming wealthy.

In order to go into home ownership the right way – by having a plan before building your tower, as Christ said – you need to learn how the numbers work and have a budget. First, examine your debt-to-income ratio. Understand the maximum percentage of your gross income (before taxes) that a lender will accept as the monthly mortgage payment. Understand the maximum percentage of your gross income for all debt payments.

When lenders consider a mortgage loan for you, they will consider your installment loans. To them, installment loans are counted when the loan payoff is longer than 10 months. That's why it is good to have the least amount of debt you can when you are looking at buying a home.

Remember: Once you buy a house, you can always buy a car; but once you buy a car, you cannot always buy a house.

Building wealth is a defensive strategy, so you need to be proactive when you are working on a goal like owning a home.

Loan First, Home Second

If you are ready to get into a home, the best plan is to get a loan secured and then go hunting for a home that will fit into the finances that you already have secured. What are the benefits of finding the loan first? First, you will understand the scope of the money it is going to take to get into your home, and second, you will understand what a house in your price range looks like. Getting a loan first also enables you to clean up your credit because it is through the loan process that many of us get our first glimpse of our credit reports. Finally, getting a loan first enables you to get into a better negotiating position as a buyer. If a home seller is deciding between a pair of prospective buyers, and one has a loan and one does not, it will be an easier decision for the seller. (Do note, however, that a locked-in loan will make it more difficult for you to go up in price if you are negotiating).

There are three options when it comes to getting a loan first: **pre-qualifying, pre-approval, and written commitment.**

Pre-qualifying is learning how much house you can buy based on your debt-to-income ratio. Pre-approval is when you sit down with a lender, they determine what your purchase limit is, and they start the mortgage paperwork. Finally, the written commitment is the best option because you and the mortgage company have gone through the entire loan process together; you now have the money in your pocket to shop with.

Exploring these options may be rough at first, especially if your loan amount isn't as high as you'd like it to be. But that's just a part of life. You don't always get what you want. Instead, you should pray about what you should do before you do it.

When you work on getting pre-qualified, you need to have your financial documents in order and ready to be checked out by the lender, including pay stubs, bank account information, investments, and anything else that will track the comings and goings of your money.

Once you are being considered for a pre-qualified loan, you need to make sure you don't make any drastic changes to your financial condition. Some of these mistakes can cause your loan not to be accepted or approved.

No-No's During Pre-Qualifying

Don't make a major credit purchase before completing your home purchase. Do NOT fill out any application for credit. For example, don't get so excited about purchasing a home that you start decorating even before moving in. For example, you may want to purchase new furniture, so you head down to the local furniture store, and there is the perfect couch – and it is on sale. The salesperson tells you he can hold the couch if you fill out this small simple credit application. DO NOT DO IT! So the couch is only $450. The furniture company will most likely open up a line of credit for you at

$5,000. This is a hit most people cannot afford to take on their credit report when trying to qualify for a loan.

Even more importantly, don't buy a car! Remember, once you buy a home, you can always buy a car; but once you buy a car, you can't always buy a home.

Don't move money around between accounts.

Don't let your emotions take over.

Don't become best friends with the seller. Remember your home purchase is a business transaction and not a process to be taken in a light manner.

Don't ignore your lender's requirements.

Don't overbuy. Do NOT get caught up in the graduated interest payment plan. So you found that $175,000 house and you really want it, and the loan officer tells you that you can have it at the same payment you'd pay if it were $125,000. What is going to happen is that your first year's interest rate may be 4%. Then the following year, it will go to 5% and then the next year 7%.

This is a called a 3-2-1 graduated rate. This is the very reason so many homes are in foreclosure now. In 2001 FNMA and Freddie Mac relaxed the lending requirements for homebuyers so much that anyone who held a job could get a home. People were purchasing as much as they could afford at the lower interest rate. The next year when the next step interest rate kicked in, it was hard to make the payment. Then, when the third year came around and the payment jumped again, it became impossible to make the payment. People were walking away from a home they had no down payment in and not enough equity in to recoup the cost of selling. Do not be fooled by thinking that says, "I should be making more money in a year and can make the payments," or "I look to inherit money from my uncle, and he is not in good health." Sometimes jobs don't come through, and Uncle Harry may live longer than you expect. The best piece of advice I can give you is to set a payment and live with it. If you make more money in the future, start a retirement plan, put money in your kids' college fund, or pay off the home you have early.

Don't change jobs.

But what about a better job?

There are some rules of thumb when it comes to changing jobs. The best rule is that if you are salaried or hourly employee and you are looking at a wage increase that you can count on with every paycheck, then you should definitely change jobs. The key here is stability and reliability when it comes to income. That's why changing jobs because of commission, bonuses, overtime or part-time is a bad idea – so is going from full-time to self-employment. Those could torpedo any deal you have for a home loan. If a job opportunity arises and you are considering moving, the job you move to should be in the same field you are currently in. A nurse, for example, may want to move from hospital A to hospital B for more money and different hours. Not a problem. But a nurse moving from hospital A to become a manager at a large department store is bad. A change of occupation shows a lack of stability. If you are a professional and perform a specific job (i.e., a nurse, doctor, engineer, accountant, or any profession where you specialize in a field), the bank will sometimes allow for future earnings if you have a job offer.

Credit Scores

When you are looking for a home loan, the lender will base your interest rate on a magic number: your credit score. Your credit score is calculated by a few factors: 35 percent is your payment history; 30 percent is the amount of money you currently owe; 15 percent is the length of your credit history; 10 percent is new credit that you have obtained, and the last 10 percent of the type of credit that you use. Through that formula, the three major credit agencies come up with a score, which is used to determine whether you can get a loan and, if you can, what the terms will be.

There are no time machines when it comes to credit. There

is no "Back to the Future" way to fix the mistakes you've made in the past, so if you meet any company promising to fix all of those bad marks on your credit, you need to walk away. The best way to fix your credit is to be diligent and set your house in order. Save up, pay off your bills, and then get a home loan.

House Into A Home

Once you have your outside ready, as the Scripture says, you need to make sure you are approaching your home purpose with the right spirit.

As the Scripture reads, *"Unless the Lord builds the house, its builders labor in vain. Unless the Lord watches over the city, the watchmen stand guard in vain. In vain you rise early and stay up late, toiling for food to eat - for he grants sleep to those he loves"* (Psalm 127:1-2).

You must look for God's blessing to be on your home. You also must buy your home when and how He wants you to. To buy the right way also means surrounding yourself with the right people.

First would be a real estate agent. You will be working hand-in-hand with this person, so ask around for a friend's reference or interview an agent. Be sure you ask the right questions and get references. There are different kinds of agents, so understand which kind of agent you are working with.

The final part of the deal you will learn about is closing costs. The many costs associated with finalizing your loan can get a little daunting. Among the costs are processing fees and origination fees, which deal with the paperwork of your loan. There are many other fees that can be negotiated, as well as points. One point equals one percent of the loan amount, and some companies will include that in your closing cost to bring down your amount and put another negotiating option on the table.

If you don't understand all of your fees and costs, make sure the lender or your agent explains them to you. This is when you need to be prayerful. Don't let emotions override your common sense and ability to make wise decisions. Information will empower you.

Listen to the Word, and you will see that God has laid out the ideal way for you to get a home: by working on the outside first, preparing a plan, making it right, and allowing Him to guide your decisions. Follow those instructions and you will unlock the door to your home sweet home!

CHAPTER REVIEW: YES, I WILL!

List three things you learned from this chapter that you will put into action in your life.

1. ____

When will you do it?

Immediately   Within the month   Within 6 months

Within 1 year   Within 5 years

2. ____

When will you do it?

Immediately   Within the month   Within 6 months

Within 1 year   Within 5 years

3. ____

When will you do it?

Immediately   Within the month   Within 6 months

Within 1 year   Within 5 years

Today is

____

Chapter 8
Money Babies : Investments

It's never too early to look into the future of your money. You may have a little, or you may have a lot now, but whatever you have, you want it to grow. Plus, you don't want it just to grow now; you want it to keep on growing even after you are gone.

That's why I call investments "Money Babies." If you take care of your money correctly, feed it, and care for it, it will keep on living and growing and will eventually help your family for a long time.

My grandma knew how to take care of her Money Babies, and those Money Babies took care of me.

My grandmother worked at Kelly Field in San Antonio, Texas, as a line worker. She worked from 6 a.m. until 2:30 p.m. She wasn't in management, and she didn't have an executive job, but when the time came for me to go to college, my grandmother came to me and she said, "What college are you going to?"

I had just graduated and said, "I am not prepared

to go to college." She said, "I'll tell you what. You go and find a college that you want to attend, and I will pay all your school expenses."

So I found a college, enrolled, lived on campus for 2 years, and graduated in 4. Every time my college bills would come due, I would send Grandma the invoice of my class schedule and tuition, and Grandma would write a check and send it right back to me. (And Grandma was wise because when she wrote that check, it wasn't made out to me; it was made out to the school). Grandma was so good that I would send her the invoice on Monday, and she had me the check by Wednesday or Thursday.

Grandma blessed me, and I will remember what she did for me for the rest of my life. When my children get ready to go to college, they will be getting the same treatment.

But in order to do that, you have to listen to the Word of God to increase your knowledge and have a vision of where you want your money to go and how you want it to help you reach your goals.

It all comes down to your understanding of money concepts. For example, let's consider interest: those who understand it make it; those who don't pay it.

The word *interest* may sound like trouble when you are first starting out and paying loans, but when you look forward and your money is beginning to grow, interest will be on your side. But how do you make it grow? By investing – and by planning.

Money Babies are the investments that start out small before they grow into something big and strong.

In order for those Money Babies to grow, you need to have a plan. Without a plan – whether it's a trip to Disney Land you want to take with your kids or the way you want to retire – you won't reach your goals. Without a plan to build your wealth, it will never grow and prosper like you want it to, and those Babies will never reach maturity. How do you get your wealth to grow?

Seven Ways to Build Wealth

1. First, have a vision for your life! If you look at the people who succeed, they are people with vision. Take someone like Colonel Sanders, who had a vision late in life that he was going to sell fried chicken. He went all over the country following that vision and became a great success. Your vision will keep you going, even as you experience failure. If your vision is strong and true, nothing will stand in your way. Thomas Edison had inventions fail time and time again before the light bulb turned on for him (literally!). I pray, and God determines where I need to go. If you are seeking a vision for your own life, talk to your

family, talk to God, and find it!

2. Your next step is to evaluate your financial position by looking at your net worth. You do this by comparing what you own against what you owe. If you are just starting out getting your house in order, don't be discouraged. You have net worth whether you know it or not. Arm yourself with this information, and be able to track yourself from this starting point.
3. Start building wealth RIGHT NOW! When? RIGHT NOW! How can I do that, you ask? Save your money any way you can. But don't do it without …
4. Setting measurable goals. These do not have to be huge; in fact, it works out well at first if they are smaller ones that you can accomplish. How about saving $10 this week or reducing your times eating out by one? Set the goal, and achieve it!
5. Next, you need to say "yes" to money, especially free money that you can make work to your advantage. This includes your company's benefits, your 401(k), or IRAs. If you can take advantage of the government offering a tax deduction or tax free opportunity, grab it with gusto.
6. Another way to "find" money is by being a conscious consumer who is very intentional about spending. You don't want to be a zombie when you see a flashy ad during

the Super Bowl. You don't want to be sucked in by labels that don't add anything to your clothes but a higher price tag. A shirt is a shirt is a shirt.

One thing I've discovered about rich people is they look for deals and don't spend money if they don't have to. I hate to go shopping because of what the prices look like, but you have to know there are going to be sales. Work with your spouse to keep an eye out for the best possible deals. My wife will talk to the salespeople at a store and tell them, "Call me when items are 50 percent off or more." Save your money so that you can strike when you can get the most for your money.

7. Finally, keep paying yourself! Don't forget that people who understand money *make* interest, and those who don't *pay* interest. Set aside some money in your budget for savings and investment.

Before we dive deeper into how to make our Money Babies grow, let's go to the Word and see what it says about finding your vision for the future of your money and making it into an investment that will secure your future.

When it comes to the principles of money, the Word says three things. First, play defense (*"For wisdom is a defense as money is a defense. But the excellence of knowledge is that wisdom gives life to those to have it."* Ecclesiastes 7:12). Next, use what God has given you as a foundation of your money and wisdom (*"His Lord said to him, 'Well done, good and faithful servant; you were faithful over a few things, I will make you ruler over many things. Enter into the joy of your Lord.'"* Matthew 25:21). Finally, in all that you do, be fruitful and multiply (*"Then God blessed them, and God said to them, 'Be fruitful and multiply; fill the earth and subdue it; have dominion over the fish of the sea, over the birds of the air, and over every living thing that moves on the earth.'"* Genesis 1:28).

If you want those Money Babies to multiply, first you need to find out where they come from and how to best raise them up.

Where Do Money Babies Come From?

When we talk about Money Babies, we are not talking about money that sits there and does nothing. We are talking about money that is active, that is running around doing something. Money Babies are GROWING because Money Babies are making more money. They grow through interest, capital growth, and dividends.

The best way to look at their growth spurts is to study their parents. Interest's parents in our world of Money Babies are Mr. and Mrs. Bond. When you buy bonds, you will be paid interest. Capital growth's parents are Mr. and Mrs.

Assets. When you put your money into assets, you will see a growth in value; something that was once worth $1,000 can be worth $1,500 over a few years. Finally, you can also count on Dividends to come from Mr. and Mrs. Stocks. This is money a company pays you for investing in their company.

Let's take a closer look at how these parents really work when it comes to feeding your Money Babies the food (interest, capital gains, and dividends) they need to be big and strong.

First, bonds are corporate or government IOUs that allows a company to get money from you in the short-term and pay you back over the long-term. You are the landlord who makes a bond like renting a house because you allow the company to use your money and they pay you back – with interest – over a set term.

A stock is different than a bond because you are taking ownership in a company. This ownership is represented by shares. You actually own a little piece of Microsoft or Wal-Mart or whatever company you invest in. As the value of the company rises, so does the value of your stock.

You can see how stocks grow by looking at the company's end of the year report and at graphs that show the wild ups and downs of the stock market. For many people, the risk may be too much, but for others, the risk is part of the fun of owning stocks!

There are many different ways to own stock, bonds, or other types of investments. You can buy shares in just one company or several companies that you really like and manage those purchases yourself, or you can put your money into a mutual fund. A mutual fund is an investment company which uses your money and that of many, many other people in order to buy many different kinds of stocks, bonds, and other investments. They are managed by financial professionals who spend their time researching just the right kinds of locations to invest in so you can get the biggest return, with the amount of risk you directed them to take.

Whatever investment you choose to make, do the correct investigation based on your needs. Do research on your own, hire a professional, or do both. Consider your risk tolerance, your diversification, and your needs.

My Budget, My Vision

Putting your budget and your vision down on paper will help give clarity to the decisions that you make when it comes to investments, spending, and your actions on the way to putting your house in order.

A vision keeps you focused, as it says in Habakkuk 2:2: *"Write the vision And make it plain on tablets, That he may run who reads it."*

If the people around you know your vision, it will help them support you. If your friends know you are on a budget, they won't ask you out to dinner but will help you save. If your vision and plan are consistent in your life, your decisions will actually be easier to make ("I can't afford this; it's not in my budget! I can't get a credit card; that goes against my vision!") The best thing of all is that your vision becomes central, and from it grow your goals and dreams, instead of fears.

Make goals to achieve your vision at different time increments. Is there something short-term you could do to feed those Money Babies? Find some loose change, add it to your savings, and that could total up to $15 a month. Do that as an 18-month goal, and you will end up with $270 you didn't know you had. The little things, like avoiding fees or eating in instead of eating out, can add up.

You should also make goals for your vision that are intermediate-term, from 1 to 5 years, and then long-term for 5 years and beyond. Maybe you want to get totally out of debt or fund your 401(k). Combining a good vision, a good plan of action, and a solid budget will get you there, and the investments you make will cause your Money Babies to blossom.

A Money Baby story

When it comes to making a little baby grow into a big investment, there's no better advantage than time. Take the story of Jill and Jack.

Jill invested her money at age 18 and contributed $2,000 a year between the ages of 18 and 29. She stopped after age 29 and only invested $24,000 total. Her account balance at age 67 was $1.6 million with a constant 10 percent rate of growth. Jack started his investing at age 30. He invested $4,000 a year between the ages of 30 to 67; he invested $148,000. His account balance at age 67 was $1.45 million with a constant 10 percent rate of growth. By starting earlier, Jill's Money Babies didn't take that much income ($24,000) but grew into something extraordinary at her retirement. Jack invested much more income ($148,000) and still didn't completely catch up (see charts at end of chapter).

A plan, a vision, and the time value of money make a difference when it comes to growing Money Babies.

Hurry, tell your kids right now! Invest for them. This is an example of "the sooner, the better."

We are going to have Money Babies when we put our house together.

What we will get is what is called "My House in Order!"

and we will applaud. That applause is going to be you in your paid-for house with your paid-for furniture and appliances, driving your paid-for car.

These principles will grow your Money Babies and leave a legacy of money and of knowledge. It is a blessing that you can pass on, just as my grandmother passed it on and blessed me.

CHAPTER REVIEW: YES, I WILL!

List three things you learned from this chapter that you will put into action in your life.

1. ______________________________

When will you do it?

Immediately   Within the month   Within 6 months

Within 1 year   Within 5 years

2. ______________________________

When will you do it?

Immediately   Within the month   Within 6 months

Within 1 year   Within 5 years

3. ______________________________

When will you do it?

Immediately   Within the month   Within 6 months

Within 1 year   Within 5 years

Today is

____

Investment Scenario Outcome

Proposed Interest Rate For Both Scenario's = 10%

Invest at age 18 for 12 years then stop!

Age	Years	Contribution	End of Year Value
18	1	$ 2,000	$ 2,200
19	2	$ 2,000	$ 4,620
20	3	$ 2,000	$ 7,282
21	4	$ 2,000	$ 10,210
22	5	$ 2,000	$ 13,431
23	6	$ 2,000	$ 16,974
24	7	$ 2,000	$ 20,872
25	8	$ 2,000	$ 25,159
26	9	$ 2,000	$ 29,875
27	10	$ 2,000	$ 35,062
28	11	$ 2,000	$ 40,769
29	12	$ 2,000	$ 47,045
30	13	$ -	$ 51,750
31	14	$ -	$ 56,925
32	15	$ -	$ 62,617
33	16	$ -	$ 68,879
34	17	$ -	$ 75,767
35	18	$ -	$ 83,344
36	19	$ -	$ 91,678
37	20	$ -	$ 100,846
38	21	$ -	$ 110,931
39	22	$ -	$ 122,024
40	23	$ -	$ 134,226
41	24	$ -	$ 147,649
42	25	$ -	$ 162,414
43	26	$ -	$ 178,655
44	27	$ -	$ 196,520
45	28	$ -	$ 216,172
46	29	$ -	$ 237,790
47	30	$ -	$ 261,569
48	31	$ -	$ 287,726
49	32	$ -	$ 316,498
50	33	$ -	$ 348,148
51	34	$ -	$ 382,963
52	35	$ -	$ 421,259
53	36	$ -	$ 463,385
54	37	$ -	$ 509,723
55	38	$ -	$ 560,696
56	39	$ -	$ 616,765
57	40	$ -	$ 678,442
58	41	$ -	$ 746,286
59	42	$ -	$ 820,915
60	43	$ -	$ 903,006
61	44	$ -	$ 993,307
62	45	$ -	$ 1,092,637
63	46	$ -	$ 1,201,901
64	47	$ -	$ 1,322,091
65	48	$ -	$ 1,454,300
66	49	$ -	$ 1,599,730
Total Contributions		$	24,000
Future Value		$	1,599,730

Invest at age 30 for 37 years until retirement

Age	Years	Contribution	End of Year Value
18	1	$ -	$ -
19	2	$ -	$ -
20	3	$ -	$ -
21	4	$ -	$ -
22	5	$ -	$ -
23	6	$ -	$ -
24	7	$ -	$ -
25	8	$ -	$ -
26	9	$ -	$ -
27	10	$ -	$ -
28	11	$ -	$ -
29	12	$ -	$ -
30	13	$ 4,000	$ 4,400
31	14	$ 4,000	$ 9,240
32	15	$ 4,000	$ 14,564
33	16	$ 4,000	$ 20,420
34	17	$ 4,000	$ 26,862
35	18	$ 4,000	$ 33,949
36	19	$ 4,000	$ 41,744
37	20	$ 4,000	$ 50,318
38	21	$ 4,000	$ 59,750
39	22	$ 4,000	$ 70,125
40	23	$ 4,000	$ 81,537
41	24	$ 4,000	$ 94,091
42	25	$ 4,000	$ 107,900
43	26	$ 4,000	$ 123,090
44	27	$ 4,000	$ 139,799
45	28	$ 4,000	$ 158,179
46	29	$ 4,000	$ 178,397
47	30	$ 4,000	$ 200,636
48	31	$ 4,000	$ 225,100
49	32	$ 4,000	$ 252,010
50	33	$ 4,000	$ 281,611
51	34	$ 4,000	$ 314,172
52	35	$ 4,000	$ 349,989
53	36	$ 4,000	$ 389,388
54	37	$ 4,000	$ 432,727
55	38	$ 4,000	$ 480,400
56	39	$ 4,000	$ 532,840
57	40	$ 4,000	$ 590,524
58	41	$ 4,000	$ 653,976
59	42	$ 4,000	$ 723,774
60	43	$ 4,000	$ 800,551
61	44	$ 4,000	$ 885,006
62	45	$ 4,000	$ 977,907
63	46	$ 4,000	$ 1,080,097
64	47	$ 4,000	$ 1,192,507
65	48	$ 4,000	$ 1,316,158
66	49	$ 4,000	$ 1,452,174
Total Contributions		$	148,000
Future Value		$	1,452,174

Investment Scenario Outcome

Proposed Interest Rate For Both Scenario's = 10%

Invest at age 18 for 12 years then stop!

Age	Years	Contribution	End of Year Value
18	1	**$ 4,000**	$ 4,400
19	2	$ 4,000	$ 9,240
20	3	$ 4,000	$ 14,564
21	4	$ 4,000	$ 20,420
22	5	$ 4,000	$ 26,862
23	6	$ 4,000	$ 33,949
24	7	$ 4,000	$ 41,744
25	8	$ 4,000	$ 50,318
26	9	$ 4,000	$ 59,750
27	10	$ 4,000	$ 70,125
28	11	$ 4,000	$ 81,537
29	12	$ 4,000	$ 94,091
30	13	$ -	$ 103,500
31	14	$ -	$ 113,850
32	15	$ -	$ 125,235
33	16	$ -	$ 137,758
34	17	$ -	$ 151,534
35	18	$ -	$ 166,688
36	19	$ -	$ 183,356
37	20	$ -	$ 201,692
38	21	$ -	$ 221,861
39	22	$ -	$ 244,047
40	23	$ -	$ 268,452
41	24	$ -	$ 295,297
42	25	$ -	$ 324,827
43	26	$ -	$ 357,310
44	27	$ -	$ 393,041
45	28	$ -	$ 432,345
46	29	$ -	$ 475,579
47	30	$ -	$ 523,137
48	31	$ -	$ 575,451
49	32	$ -	$ 632,996
50	33	$ -	$ 696,296
51	34	$ -	$ 765,925
52	35	$ -	$ 842,518
53	36	$ -	$ 926,770
54	37	$ -	$ 1,019,447
55	38	$ -	$ 1,121,391
56	39	$ -	$ 1,233,530
57	40	$ -	$ 1,356,884
58	41	$ -	$ 1,492,572
59	42	$ -	$ 1,641,829
60	43	$ -	$ 1,806,012
61	44	$ -	$ 1,986,613
62	45	$ -	$ 2,185,274
63	46	$ -	$ 2,403,802
64	47	$ -	$ 2,644,182
65	48	$ -	$ 2,908,600
66	49	$ -	$ 3,199,460
Total Contributions		$	48,000
Future Value		$	3,199,460

Invest at age 30 for 37 years until retirement

Age	Years	Contribution	End of Year Value
18	1	$ -	$ -
19	2	$ -	$ -
20	3	$ -	$ -
21	4	$ -	$ -
22	5	$ -	$ -
23	6	$ -	$ -
24	7	$ -	$ -
25	8	$ -	$ -
26	9	$ -	$ -
27	10	$ -	$ -
28	11	$ -	$ -
29	12	$ -	$ -
30	13	**$ 4,000**	$ 4,400
31	14	$ 4,000	$ 9,240
32	15	$ 4,000	$ 14,564
33	16	$ 4,000	$ 20,420
34	17	$ 4,000	$ 26,862
35	18	$ 4,000	$ 33,949
36	19	$ 4,000	$ 41,744
37	20	$ 4,000	$ 50,318
38	21	$ 4,000	$ 59,750
39	22	$ 4,000	$ 70,125
40	23	$ 4,000	$ 81,537
41	24	$ 4,000	$ 94,091
42	25	$ 4,000	$ 107,900
43	26	$ 4,000	$ 123,090
44	27	$ 4,000	$ 139,799
45	28	$ 4,000	$ 158,179
46	29	$ 4,000	$ 178,397
47	30	$ 4,000	$ 200,636
48	31	$ 4,000	$ 225,100
49	32	$ 4,000	$ 252,010
50	33	$ 4,000	$ 281,611
51	34	$ 4,000	$ 314,172
52	35	$ 4,000	$ 349,989
53	36	$ 4,000	$ 389,388
54	37	$ 4,000	$ 432,727
55	38	$ 4,000	$ 480,400
56	39	$ 4,000	$ 532,840
57	40	$ 4,000	$ 590,524
58	41	$ 4,000	$ 653,976
59	42	$ 4,000	$ 723,774
60	43	$ 4,000	$ 800,551
61	44	$ 4,000	$ 885,006
62	45	$ 4,000	$ 977,907
63	46	$ 4,000	$ 1,080,097
64	47	$ 4,000	$ 1,192,507
65	48	$ 4,000	$ 1,316,158
66	49	$ 4,000	$ 1,452,174
Total Contributions		$	148,000
Future Value		$	1,452,174

Chapter 9
Leave A Legacy : Estate Planning

Have you thought about death today? Not really a comfortable subject, is it? Most of us like to walk around and think of death as something that happens to other people. But it *is* going to happen to you.

So as you come to the end of your financial plan, it's time to start thinking about the legacy you are going to leave your family and whether you are going to leave them financial and mental stress after you die. You can't wait until you are older to take action when it comes to your end-of-life decisions. These decisions aren't just limited to a will. You also need to make choices about what happens when your health takes a poor turn. Think of the Terry Schaivo case, where the ambiguity of her decisions took her case all the way to Congress. Having a living will or health directive would have solved the entire situation.

You have a chance to make a difference in your family's financial success. But you can't procrastinate.

DO IT TODAY!

When you start the conversation with your family about where your estate plan fits into your goals and vision, you need to begin by asking yourself some questions:

* What are my assets, and what is their approximate value?
* Whom do I want to receive those assets – and when?
* Who should manage those assets if I cannot, either during my lifetime or after my death?
* Who should have the responsibility for the care of my minor children if I become incapacitated or die?
* If I cannot take care of myself, who should make decisions on my behalf concerning my care and welfare?

The first question you ask yourself is about your assets. These are the items that you have of value, that are worth more than you owe, and that are among the possessions that you will pass on as part of your legacy.

In the Word of God, the Lord asked people to take stock of what they have because He knew that they would need to be tended to after we leave this life. In Proverbs 27:23-24, the Bible says, *"Be diligent to know the state of your flocks and attend to your herds; for riches are not forever, nor does a crown endure to all generations."* The Word also compels us to walk with God as we make these decisions because we will be walking with Him daily when we join Him in Heaven. If you are walking with the Lord, following the vision He has laid out for you up to your final moments on Earth, then your plan is truly blessed. *"For the Lord God is a sun and shield; The Lord will give grace and glory; no good thing will be withheld from those who walk uprightly. O Lord of hosts, blessed is the man who trusts in you"* (Psalm 84:11-12).

Do I Need Life Insurance?

This is an important question because some very basic needs come along with envisioning a future for your family after you die. Before you die, you need to think about how to replace your income.

What is your family going to do about the bills that come after you have gone?

I once knew a family who was burying their father. They had the funeral, and at the funeral, an offering was given to the family, which is very unusual. After the funeral, no one went to the graveside. The morticians took the body, put it back into the hearse, took it to the funeral home, put it into the vault, and left it there. The family did not have enough money to pay for the burial of their father. Think about that anguish.

That is why you need life insurance: for burial expenses, for college expenses, for medical bills, and for the mortgage. Those bills will still need to be paid if you die.

How Much Life Insurance Do You Need?

A simple rule of thumb in life insurance says you need to have 10 to 12 times your annual salary. So, for instance, if you make $30,000 a year, you need to have between $300,000 and $360,000 worth of life insurance.

The cost is going to vary based on the kind of life insurance you purchase (term, whole life, universal life, etc.) and the needs you have. Term insurance is always going to be cheapest because it only lasts a set period of time. This is the way to go when you are young and don't have many assets built up.

Life insurance is a balancing act. If you have enough assets to cover the replacement of your family's income or to provide for your burial, then you don't need insurance. If you don't have enough assets to cover those expenses, then you need it. Look at your vision, and see what the length of time will be to get you from Point A to Point B, and that can be the length of time for your term insurance.

Term insurance is temporary. If you want a different type of policy, you can look into cash value insurance, which typically lasts your lifetime.

You want to have enough insurance just in case something happens and you don't have the assets to help your family. Some people only want to have enough insurance to cover their family until their kids grow up. What you need to do is shop around.

Look around the internet, and check local agents as well as your place of employment to see what insurance is best for you.

Wills, Trusts and Estate Planning

Another big end of life question is about wills. A will is a legal document which outlines what you want done for your family and with your possessions after you die.

Do you need a will? If you want to leave a legacy, you should have one. If you want your wishes respected, you should have one, too.

People need to have a will if they have minor children and want to determine who takes care of them. Another very valid reason for having a will is that when a loved one dies, when a parent dies, or when a spouse dies, a difficult time is made much easier if the deceased person has left behind a will that tells everyone exactly what his or her wishes were regarding his or her estate.

Then, no one has to agonize over what Mom would have wanted or what Dad would have wanted.

Also, leaving things up in the air can create turmoil within the family because different family members want different things.

Don't make the mistake of thinking you don't have enough of an estate to worry about a will. If you have a home, a car, a checking account, or furniture, those are all assets that you can leave behind. Heirlooms like family Bibles or china that children may want also need to be taken into account.

Again, a will is especially needed if you have minor children. If you and your spouse were to die at the same time, you don't want to leave it up to the state to determine who will raise your children. You want those wishes known and followed. Also, if you have minor children and are leaving them money, you can set up a trust that will name a trustee who will help your children use the money wisely. You can even decide when they receive it as adults. It doesn't have to be 18 but can be whatever age you choose.
You decide when they will be ready to receive the money that is waiting for them.

If you have any major changes happen during your life, you are going to need to update your will. Be sure to keep that in mind when you have more children and as your wealth grows. Unfortunately, even if you have a will, you will not be able to avoid the probate system, which is set up to deal with the transfer of assets from your estate to the people you named in your will. This can hang your assets up for some time, but it is better than the alternative of dying without a will. You DON'T want to do that!

One way to avoid probate is to set up a trust. If you have assets, a trust can make things a lot easier since it helps your estate avoid the large fees that come with probate. If the trust owns your assets and not you, your family will get a lot of ease and benefit at the time of your death.

Two other parts of estate planning are an Advance Directive for Health Care or Living Will, and a Durable Power of Attorney.

The Living Will comes into play when your life is being maintained by life support systems. So that your family will not have a difficult decision to make, you can sign a living will while still mentally competent, outlining what your wishes are in certain medical scenarios and sharing those with your love ones.

Also recommended is a Durable Power of Attorney, which is a document in which you can appoint someone to handle your financial matters in the event that you are mentally or physically unable to do so. The great thing about a Durable Power of Attorney is that it does not become effective until you are determined by a doctor to be incapacitated.

We pray that God protects and heals your body in such times, but we cannot avoid the fact that all of us will eventually die. God has given us these legal tools while we are on earth to protect ourselves and our families and make the vision He has for us come to be.

CHAPTER REVIEW: YES, I WILL!

List three things you learned from this chapter that you will put into action in your life.

1. ____

When will you do it?

Immediately   Within the month   Within 6 months

Within 1 year   Within 5 years

2. ____

When will you do it?

Immediately   Within the month   Within 6 months

Within 1 year   Within 5 years

3. ____

When will you do it?

Immediately   Within the month   Within 6 months

Within 1 year   Within 5 years

Today is

____

Epilogue
My Personal Story

All these years later, I will never forget the day. July 4, 1984.

The day my parents gave me my independence. They were tired of my attitude. They were tired of my constant complaints. They wanted me to learn that life is what I make it and not what someone else can do for me.

I will never forget.

I had no place to live. I had no food to eat. All the clothes I had were in the back of my car.

I drove down the highway, wondering what I would do next and where I would go. Then, I saw The Cross.

There it was, all lit up on top of one of the local hospitals. I pulled into the parking lot, got out, and found the hospital chapel.

And I cried, asking the Lord, "What have I done?" I asked God to forgive me.

The next couple of days, I stayed in the hospital

parking lot. I washed my face and brushed my teeth in the water fountain.

Eventually, I got myself together and asked my parents to forgive me.

At the time, I thought gaining my independence abruptly was the worst thing that ever happened to me, but later, I found out it was also the best thing that ever happened to me.

Not too long after, I spoke with my grandmother, who offered to pay for my college. I worked hard, finished in 4 years, and then got married.

In that whole experience, I realized some things. I was very rebellious. I was very hard-headed. I was stiff-necked and selfish.

But more than anything, I realized I needed a true relationship with God in my life.

Have you ever seen those nature specials on TV where the mother eagle is trying to teach the baby eagles to fly? In that world, there's not much time for instruction. You either fly, or you don't. So the mother eagle just kicks the babies out of the nest. While they are dropping, they'd better learn to fly!

That's what my parents did for me. I wasn't wise enough to realize how I was acting, so they forced me to learn to fly on my own.

Now I have more than I ever imagined I would have,

physically, financially, and spiritually, and all of it is God's blessing.

But the biggest blessing of all is that I have Jesus Christ as my personal Savior.

I hope that you've read this book and gotten some good, practical tips out of it. I hope it was useful to you.

But more than that, I hope that you see that God has a plan and a vision for your life. He has laid out the instructions for how to get your house in order in his holy Word and through the life of his Son, Jesus Christ.

What is my vision? That everyone who reads this book would strengthen their relationship with God or become saved.

The title of this book comes from the story of King Hezekiah, whom God told to get his house in order before he died because he was going to die soon.

That's a truth we all must face: None of us will live in this world forever. We can put our house in order and leave a legacy for our children, but we will still die.

But if we accept Jesus Christ as our Savior, we will spend the rest of eternity in the richest place there is – with God in Heaven.

And, as we've talked about all this money and financial information, we end with the greatest gift of all: a *free* gift that anyone can pray for and accept – the forgiveness of God through faith in Jesus.

As is written in the book of Romans, "That if you confess with your mouth, 'Jesus is Lord,' and believe in your heart that God raised him from the dead, you will be saved. For it is with your heart that you believe and are justified, and it is with your mouth that you confess and are saved."

If you have prayed to God and accepted Jesus as your Savior, please note your decision below.

I confess my sins and accept Jesus as my personal Savior.

Name ________________________________

Date ____________

Keep God in your heart, on your lips, in your vision, and in your action.

Follow His plan to get your house and your heart in order. Because if you do, you will find yourself shouting with joy, just as I have so many times.

YES, I CAN!

YES, I CAN!

YES, I CAN!

"I can do all things through Christ who strengthens me"

Philippians 4:13

- Keith

"To God be all the glory!"

"Yes, I Can Set My House in Order!" is a program developed by Keith Carter for churches and businesses that want to help their congregations or employees set their houses in order. Keith is available to lead workshops which complement this book. There are eight workshops in the series, and they build on each other. To contact Keith, you can call him at 1-888-580-0937 or at 405-330-6431.

Keith is a financial consultant and ordained minister who lives in Edmond, Oklahoma, with his wife and three children.
Keith graduated from the University of Central Oklahoma where he received a bachelor's and master's degree in finance. He has taught corporate finance at Langston University and personal finance at Oklahoma State University. He has completed his Registered Financial Consultant certification and has more than 16 years experience as a presenter of educational, financial, and Christian workshops.

Keith is the president of I AM THIRD Financial Services (God First, Family Second, and I am Third) with offices in Oklahoma and Texas, where he provides financial planning, asset management, and retirement planning services.

I AM THIRD's mission statement is as follows:
To educate financially and spiritually.
To encourage all.
To protect and grow my clients' assets and be spiritually conscious in all decisions.

The next page is a certificate for you to cut away from your book and use to mark the date when you set your house in order. "Est." is an abbreviation for the word *established*. I encourage you to put the certificate in a nice frame and hang it on the wall or put on your desk. This can be a constant reminder to you that ...

"Yes, I Can Set My House in Order!"

Yes, I Can

Set My House In Order!™

... "Thus says the LORD; 'Set your house in order, for you shall die, and not live.'" 2 Kings 20:1b (NKJV)

I have a vision for my life.

My house is not stressful; my house is successful!

color 8 x 11 copy of this page can be downloaded from *www.YesICanSetMyHouseInOrder.com*

Yes, I Can

Set My House In Order! ™

Your Guide To Building A Financially Successful Life

written by

Keith Carter, RFC, MBA

CPSIA information can be obtained
at www.ICGtesting.com
Printed in the USA
FFOW02n1223070917
39701FF

9 780615 270883